Vernal Strokes

Vernal Strokes

Latha Prem Sakhya

PARTRIDGE
A Penguin Random House Company

Print information available on the last page.

To order additional copies of this book, contact
Partridge India
000 800 10062 62
orders.india@partridgepublishing.com

www.partridgepublishing.com/india

Latha Prem Sakhya

Latha Prem Sakhya (Born, Latha Prem Kumari B. on 21 January 1959) hails from Neyyoor in the Kanyakumari district of Tamilnadu, India. She did her school education in the Holy Angel's Convent, and college in His Highness the Maharaja's College for Women, Thiruvananthapuram (Kerala). She was the former Head and Associate Professor of the Department of English of Mar Thoma College for Women, Perumbavoor in Kerala, India. At present she leads a retired life with her husband Yogeendra Sakhya k. at Perumbavoor. Her only daughter, Dr. Jennifer Sakhya, resides with her husband and two children.

Memory Rain, her first collection of poems, was published in 2008. Her second book **Nature at My Doorstep**(2011) is a compilation of her poems, musings, sketches and paintings. Latha in her poignant outpouring **Vernal Strokes**, reaches the hearts of the readers, awakening them to a world of beauty and anguish. Ecstasy and agony dwell hand in hand with each other; yet the quest does not end there – her words are a mirror to the world of the lonely, the sick and the suffering. She draws us into her universe which is easy to identify with and be a part of. Her poems reflect a candour and transparency which can shock the readers out of their apathy. In this era of haste and race against one another and time, her poems are a refreshing mirror into life in all its myriad forgotten forms – the small and the simple are brought before us; gripping in their reality. **Vernal Strokes** is a clarion call to the reader to wake up to a world that soothes, reminds and nourishes with beauty, pain, and hope. A close friend of nature, Latha shares her unhappiness in humanity's disregard for mother earth. To those of us 'deafened by the roar of materialistic living' these poems bring hope. She paints her 'magic in the air' with her words – a magic that does not disappear, but lingers within the reader.

By,
Prema Nair

Dedicated to
God Almighty
And to
You

Contents

Preface

That it will never come again
Is what makes life so sweet.
                              Emily Dickinson

Life is full of colour, warmth and light, and man, ever since his creation has been striving to capture it and make it a part of his life to attain happiness. These poems, penned from 1990 for my personal delight are an attempt - to capture some of the treasured moments of evanescent life. They are more personal than political and express my own strong beliefs and convictions

For me, writing poems has been an exercise for a fuller life, a means to utilize all God given gifts and a way of expressing my emotional response to life. These poems have grown with me in thought and content and have empowered me to the extent that I have transcended the fear of everything that restraints me as a woman, including, the fear of being jostled out of life into invisibility. They have given me a space to exist as a human being enjoying the minutiae of life.

I feel like Pablo Neruda about the arrival of poetry in my life and with it my latent love for painting. Like him I don't know how it happened but when it happened, they gifted me with a new life. There was a time in my life when I was running away from life itself, searching for some place where I could hide myself. Life was overwhelming me. Living had become an arduous task for me. But deep inside a tiny voice was urging me to snap out of it. On the one side I knew I was sliding down into an abyss of unfathomable darkness where I found no hope or succor. On the other, stood a whole world of beauty where I had to live only in the moment, taking life as it came, as one rides the waves. I had only to make a choice and one day choosing to look out through the windows of my tortured soul, I perceived beauty and poetry in everything around me.

And I became a new being, I lived momentously, neither looking back nor concerned about the future. I learned to perceive beyond the surface of things and to read the silence and to interpret the negative space. I began to sing about myself, my little joys and sorrows and the buoy of my life – My God – whom I found I could lean upon without any inhibition, never worried of rebuff, even when I fell short of His expectations. In Him I found a shoulder to cry upon and a friend who never failed me. And everything changed for me. I found joy in giving love and that sufficed and it drew me closer to my Almighty and I wrote passionately about everything that pulled at my heart strings.

Latha Prem Sakhya

Acknowledgement

"Alone we can do so little, together we can do so much" said Helen Keller and I feel it's a truth. This book would not have happened if my loved ones did not ask me aren't you writing, if they had not reminded me of it on and off, if they had not given me time and space to work on, if they had not chosen and selected for me keeping aside their leisure, if they had not spend time for reading, writing and editing, if they had not pointed out the errors, if they had not encouraged at every turn. Yes, this book would never have happened but for the joint effort of all those who love and support me. And I feel the best has been churned out.

I begin by thanking my Almighty God, my benevolent creator, for His infinite blessings upon me, which I experienced at every step of its creation.

I am filled with heartfelt gratitude to my mentor, Professor K.I. Jacob, former Principal of Mar Thoma College For Women, Perumbavoor, where I taught for thirty years. He has always been a model for me as a teacher and as a wonderful, sensitive and empathetic human being. He spent his valuable time for helping me to choose the best poems for this edition and also for analyzing the poems as he had understood them, which was a booster for me to bring out this publication without any doubt as to its appeal for reader

I profusely thank, from the bottom of my heart, Dr Sujeesh C.K, Associate Professor of the Department of English, Sree Sankara College, Kalady, whose sensitive and empathetic **Foreword** has become an asset to my book. His stimulating, enlightening and prized suggestions for perfecting the manuscript including the cover page, and other aspects of the book had aided me much to shape the book to the present form.

I am extremely grateful to Prema J. Nair and Shimi M. my friends, for being there for me to do all the odd jobs related to editing and shaping the manuscript to its final stage. I am indebted to Prema for her sincere contribution about **Vernal Strokes**. I specially thank my beloved nephew, Reny M. John who promptly wrote the blurb. I also thank my dear friends who helped with the Previews of **Vernal Strokes.**

I thank my Publisher Partridge India; special thanks to Ms. karen Jimenez, Publishing Consultant whose encouraging words urged me to hasten up my task for publishing my third book, and a big thanks to Mr Pohar Baruah, my Publishing Services Associate, always calm and soft aiding me with the correct guidance, support and assurance which I needed for completing the book. A word of sincere thanks to the Partridge India team of designers for the beautiful cover art and for the apt lay out of the interior pages.

I thank all my teachers and all the guiding forces in my life, my friends who stand with me, my siblings and all my relatives for supporting me with love and prayers through the good times as well as the challenging periods of my life and to my nieces and nephews for sustaining me with their love.

I am indebted to my late father John Bright and my paternal grandmother Kanakammal Martin, for being major influences in my formative years and making me what I am.

I am full of appreciation and gratitude to my mother Mrs Flower Bright, for lighting my path daily and being a source of perennial inspiration.

Words are scant for thanking my adorable family, my husband Yogeendra Sakhya who is a strong pillar of strength gently supporting me at every turn, my daughter Jennifer Sakhya, who helped me with the cover, my son in-law Lenju Paul and my two grandsons baby Julian and baby Juan, who enliven my life each day with their loving presence and overwhelm me with their love, which keeps me going.

Finally I am grateful to the whole universe and to all living creatures and non-living objects in it, which are my constant sources of joy and inspiration.

Latha Prem Sakhya

Foreword

Poetry should come as natural as a leaf to a tree, says John Keats. It comes just as natural to a woman. Latha Prem Sakhya's volume of poems **Vernal Strokes** conceives a female centred conception of life, which subsumes the whole earth -- its forms, colours, odours, pangs, pleasures, hopes, dreams, failures, chill and heat, interwoven together, each intrinsically blended with the other. The conception may simply be called Earth Spirit or Gaea Earth. The poems may rightly be called Earth Songs, celebrating the myriad facets of the single, life preserving, glorious Gaea Earth. It presupposes the cyclical rhythm of generation, regeneration and degeneration as the inevitable patterns of existence. Her use of linguistic devices intensifies and solidifies relationships.

The earth songs include "portaits" of a wide range of earthly beings that live in close harmony with the rhythm and essence of nature. "New Nest" lights up the tiny one's first flight from the nest under the vigilant parents:

"The little one circled in the air
With swan like grace
Under the watchful eyes
Of the adoring pair."

The struggle of the female is vividly drawn in "Wild Woman."

"Trusting her heart, listening

To the small guiding voice inside -
Primitive, yet authentic and true to self
Doing what gives joy - laughing, crying,
Waltzing, bawling, sniffing,
Gnarling, scratching, loving,
Running free, snoozing
The female soul;

The poet is enamoured by the magic spell of nature in "Nature's Magic Spell."

Spying on the silvery fishes,
Playful water snakes and watchful herons,
I sat ensconced
In Nature's magic spell."

The black and white feathery singer's portrait is seen in "Notes of Joy." The tiny bird in the lawn

". . . With his inner joy,
Proclaimed to the world -
Through peals and peals of melody."

"Minnows" is a poem that tries to contrast the simple life of the animal world with the complex nature of human life. In "Extended Family," there is a celebration of extending or widening the horizons of individual's concept of family. In the poet's extended family, there are a lot of members -- both human and non human. The bird of ill omen also is a privileged member of this family, as seen in "Lord of the Night." earth poems secretly admire the caressing Sun. "The dancing Sun beam caressing the stream/ And sweeping her into his golden arms" ("The Rill").

Earth songs are composed in a language that has a rare lucidity through which the poet successfully expresses the variegated moods of the "characters" (the flora and fauna) that are portrayed. A variety of emotional facets of Gaea Earth can be seen in Earth Poems. The tree in "Tree" is a "perennial emblem of of prayer" and is "sans cast, creed, or positions." "The Rill" is full of

"Fishes flashing their silver scales.
The water fowls playing hide and seek
In the coverts of rocks and ridges."

A felled tree in "Anguish" is a "weird tree in some ghostly fantasy." an uprooted tree in "Shaddock" is consoled thus,

"I heard you weep earth child
As you lay uprooted on your side-"

There are moments where the poet, along with ecstasy and agony, captures the revolt of nature, and the whole earth. The poem "Wild Furies" gives expression to such a revolt:

"The foaming, frothing ocean-
Million, Wild, stampeding horses,
Attacked ferociously, the benign, calm shore.

....

Gigantic dragon waves
Swallowed land and people;
Satiated, spat out the residue."

The poet is ashamed of herself as a representative of the betrayers, defiling and destroying the Earth. "Shall I Let Her Go?" reveals the guilt of the poet for the inability to help a female dog in need. However, there are occasional moments of a sense of relief and security which tells us that many of the human children of Gaea Earth do care for her and the siblings. Humiliation and freedom from captivity are narrated in "Sans Fangs, Sans Teeth." the snake in the monologue says that it takes refuge in the basket, "Where I coiled tightly to sleep/ To forget man-hurt and humiliation." at last, when it is freed in a jungle, it got a new life.

"The earthy woody smell
Assailed me and I slid away
In a lightning flash
In search of a new home
Far away from humans."

Ultimately, Earth is a woman, and the poem "What am I Now" is lament of the worn out mother:

"Senile, losing control of body and spirit
I wonder! Do my children,
My earthlings, see my struggle?"

From Gaea Earth, a number of poems in the volume take us to the life and destiny of every woman. The poems of this category evoke the infinite facets of woman. The poems, in this sense, may be understood to sketch Gynoscapes. Woman is formed out of the essential and vital part of the Earth, yet is different; in that woman is a separate, individual organism. This dichotomy characterizes the poems of Gynoscapes.

Woman's plight is more complex than that of the Earth, chiefly as a sustainer and procurer; and on the other, woman is exposed to a number of additional experiences as a human being. Woman is a combination of Gaea Earth and an individual human.

The poems of Gynoscapes sketch out the trajectory of woman from child hood, passing through various stages, to old age. The facets are brought out through an array of profiles. As a child, she comes "With laughing eyes, pouting lips, and a lanky body" and, as seen in "My Child," she is "A doe, you came nuzzling into my heart/ Making me your willing slave." when she grows up,

"The lava of slavish life erupts
Sputtering, spewing, spurting-
The assertion of self." ("Girl")

The child's anguish grieves the mother in "Spark,"

"Was there no positive
Spark, a speck, a flicker,
To keep you going, my child?"

Moments of extreme agony torments the mother,

"A hermit - you crawled into yourself;
Dwelling in the dark subconscious.
Your arrival in the juvenile home
Was a blessing, but short lived. ("Spark")

In youth, love and unrequited love haunt her,

Did I tell you
The moment I saw you
My heart missing a beat
Sank to the pit of my being.
Did I tell you?
That I love you

A love doomed to death
Like a still -born babe
In the womb?" ("Did I Tell You?")
However, with love, and relationship with the
opposite sex brings moments of confrontation as
seen in "So Near, Yet So Far,"

"Riding the passions
Curbing and harnessing wild desires
In the caves of the subconscious."

Or, "My heart rend-with tiny, tiny, tears./Have
become holes too big for patching up." ("Patching
Up"). Entry into the married life and the role of the
mother, the career, the confrontations domestic and
otherwise, get portrayed in a precise language. "A
Mother's Day" describes the toil of the working
mother from four in the morning till late night. The
only consolation beside the loved one also is often
denied:

"But often these too are strained
By flaring disagreements,
Quickly smothered
By fatigue and sleep - a blessing."

"The Trapped Bird" compares the woman/the
mother in the patriarchal fold to a bird fallen into
a trap.

"Abject beings, self-effacing doormats,
Shaped by patriarchal hegemony."

The domestic struggle, the circus and the sacrifice
go on:

I brushed not my teeth
In fear that a drop of water

Be swallowed to defeat the cause." ("To Live Freely")

However, the sacrifices are not recognized nor become fruitful. In the end, the plight is painful and hollow:

"A drying spring, battling to ooze out,

To cling on to life

With odds heavily ranged against her." ("Drying Spring")

In "Temptation," the woman's thoughts about committing suicide get expressed:

"The thirst to drink,

From the sweet cup of oblivion-

Was very enticing."

"Waiting" is a sketch of the old mother waiting eagerly for the man to turn up:

"But now all alone in the big house

I strain, keeping still to capture

Your gentle footfall, on the gravel."

Often the thoughts about mother and grandmother console the woman. Here the destiny of the woman comes full circle:

"You listened to my childish woes

And filled with confidence,

I thrived on your infinite fund of stories-

And rode on fancies wings." ("Paattie" Granny)

You rocked me on your lap

Satiating me with stories infinite." ("Rocking Lap")

"Perennial Inspiration" is the old woman's journey to the mother's memories, and "Bereft" leaves the woman

"Burning Pyre,
Bereft wife
Bewildered children."

As the whole universe is seen in a drop of water, the three lines encapsulate the life of woman.

There is an inner struggle within the woman which arises from the conflict between the demands of the elements of sustainer and procurer that she inherited from Gaea Earth, and from the contradictory in her that she got from the individual priorities she is expected to make.

Reading the poems of Latha Prem Sakhya gives one the presence of a living spirit looking at everything around, with a gaze which is warm, fresh and agile. The anthology takes the reader to a heart - compassionate, in communion with nature, where all the living and the non living grow into a hallowed existence. These are indeed words from the heart - transparent, sensitive, and sincere, coupled with the characteristic warmth of a woman.

Dr. Sujeesh C.K.

Words from My Heart

Words from my heart
Are my only possession!
Words squeezed out of ecstasy and agony-
To paint the purplish blue sky
The angry clouds driven by gale;
To sketch the beauty of nature
And her passionate reprisals;
To trace the sensuous curves of a woman,
Or the Adonis body of a man;
Their ardent lives!
To portray the innocence
Of a new born babe;
To mourn the loss of celestial knowledge,
To reflect the twinkle in smiling eyes;
To revel in joy; to sob in anguish,
Words from my heart
Are all I have.

Growing Up

Growing up has taught me
Many things - sweet and bitter.
I cherish the sweet ones,
And dump the others.
In the attic of my soul.

But, when I am down and unhappy
When my mind is storm-ridden,
They crawl one by one-
Down the stairs of the attic
To stone my spirit-
With taunts and fears infinite
I had tried desperately to forget.

Down Memory Lane

Going down memory lane,
I came to my old homestead-
Where, for seventeen summers
I was nurtured.

The old rambling house, with its spacious rooms;
The sweeping land; the gigantic tamarind trees-
Four great pillars- sentry like
Guarding the terrain.

The second one, nearest to my homestead -
Our favourite haunt! My siblings
And I, with childish enthusiasm, played
Making doll houses and keeping house.

Oh, it was such fun then!
No care, no worries,
Only innocent mirth and grief.
But alas gliding years,
Weaves a nostalgic dream
Unwinding the spool of yearning,
To regain the golden days of childhood.

Reminiscence

Nostalgic images of the past flood me-
Ensconcing me in its warmth.
Rejuvenating me with vivacity
To face the myriad headed life.

The image of a rabbit-faced ten year old,
Rushing about in white petticoat,
Urging siblings to dress hastily,
Simultaneously packing lunch and school bags.

The over laden school girl, carrying
Her infant brother, perched on her hip,
Metal box and lunch basket in her other hand,
Marching swiftly, her siblings following.

The long-haired, lanky adolescent,
Rushing to her siblings' classes in the noon,
Herding them to the dining room,
Coercing them to eat.

Scores and scores of lively images,
When life was full - an adventure,
When waking up was a thrill,
Every new day a bundle of surprise.

But now in the autumn of life,
Living, loving, serving, sacrificing,
When the thorns of life pierce and slash me,
I surface for air.

And these wistful images, overpower me,
Refreshing me with energy new
To carry on, with the same girlish zest
Each fresh day gifted to me.

Girl

Dimple cheeks, curly hair, shining eyes -
Chubby and innocent, loved and cuddled by all,
The cynosure of every eye,
You little girl!

Fleeing Time moulds you-
A butterfly, you flit through adolescence.
Blossoming womanhood-broken winged,
You wade through life,
Devoid of identity and individuality.

Chattel to one and all,
An ox pulling burden too heavy
Bestowed by God and man
Generation after generation.

One day self realization
The lava of slavish life erupts,
Sputtering, spewing, spurting -
The assertion of self,
Affirmation of individuality,
Ostracizes you-
An out caste among your own.

Why Are You So Crazy?

Why are you so crazy?
Matters negligible to others
Trouble and torment you.
What makes you so sensitive, lassie,
To others' as well as your problems?

Your face a mirror to thoughts deep,
Oft taken for granted by people close,
Unnoticed, numb and frozen, you move
Hiding your inner miseries and sorrows
Yet, sympathetic, kind, understanding.

Never hurting anyone purposefully,
Ever ready to help indiscriminately.
Yet unkind actions and rude words
Slash and prick you to hasten
To find solace in the inner den.

You forget your pain serving others.
Your beaming face belie the heartache
And the smile bedimmed by clouds dark
Rains down washing the grit and grime,
For the rainbow to shine accepting life.

Dreams

Dreams! Dreams! Dreams!
Invading the mind-
The lost babe in the wood;
The girl haunted by mother-hurt;
The freakish adolescent in quest of identity;
The alienated scholar in search
of truth and knowledge;
The blossoming woman, in pursuit of fulfillment-
All headless, grotesque figures, dancing in and out
Through the dim caverns of the subconscious.
Making me powerless- yet struggling to be free
Out of their haunting grip.

Airy Dreams

Love- beautiful, idyllic- a lily in purity.
But when tainted with lust-
The airy dreams attaining shapes,
Shatters the lovers.

But true love is like the tender breeze,
That gently kisses the flower-
Leaving it,
Swaying for more.

It is like the poignant song -
Unique and unheard.
But hummed by the lover,
In his heart.

Ideal love makes the beloved bloom
Like a flower,
And to waltz to the song,
Twinkling in the lover's eyes.

Love or Fantasy

What shall I name you?
Who came snaking into my heart?
Lying dormant for years
Like a spark waiting to be lighted.

Are you my true love?
Or are you just my fantasy?
Now turned to a nightmare?
Entangled in its octopus grip,
I fight for breath, for life-
Frightened I would be shattered -
Shards of a broken pot.

Your Love For Me

Your love for me
Is like the air I breathe,
I do not see but I feel.
It keeps me sailing
Through the myriad routines.
It gives a lilt to my steps,
Adds a tinkle to my laughter,
Softens my speech,
Fills me with generosity,
To forgive and to forget -
Even soul hurts.

Yes - your love makes me see
The hidden colours of the shining sun,
Hear the silent notes in the songs of birds,
Spy the invisible hues of flowers,
Absorb Nature's music, its infinite notes
And to sweep into my heart
The ever-changing beauty of Nature.
Yes, your love has given me
A new lease to my life.

Fortress

Your eyes are twin traitors,
Reflecting the dark passion
In your heart.

Your eyes like twin daggers,
Rip open my body
To find the veracity of my denial.

The prayer, that no clue be found
Leading to shattering catastrophe
Stands guard to the fortress of my heart and body.

Stolen Pleasures

Stolen pleasures -
Moment's darlings.
As evanescent as dew drops,
Or play of light on a cloudy day,
Cannot be treasured and cherished.
Fool she is,
Who yearns to nurture such pleasures!
Begetters of pain and sorrow.

Relationship

Gnarled roots of the tree
Desperately clinging to earth
Fearful, the least loosening
Would topple her down
To disintegrate
But, that's life.

Will You Remember Me?

Will you remember me when I am gone?
The strip of a school girl
Haunting your days
Binding you -
Ivy, intertwining,
Clinging passionately
To the stout trunk
Of your support.

So Near yet So Far

Two hearts throbbing like one
Riding the passions
Curbing and harnessing wild desires
In the caves of the subconscious.
Airy dreams wafting in
Cools the burning soul
Lit by the fire of unbridled love
Created by proximity.

A love - yearning for fulfillment
As sun beams yearn to be
In the heart of the Sun
But destined to wander
Bringing light and life to others
Very near the sun yet so far away.

Vain Love

Every thought a dagger stab,
Bleeding she lay on the torturous
Rack of unrequited love, supine.
Vignettes, hawk talons
Dug and clawed her being.

The whys of existence
Writhing, twisting, snakes
Baring fangs, poising to strike,
Evading, she wallowed
In the slough of despair.

Life stretched out her hand
Drawing her to mundane
Thousand and one things
Shelved, in her eagerness
To embrace this vain new born love.

Wailing Banshee

Love was once a red rose-
Vital and crimson; life giving blood.
But now she has pined herself out-
An Echo haunting the valleys,
Pale and wintry like the dead season
Mourning the loss of her former glory
-A wailing banshee lamenting her fall.

The empress of all virtues,
Wooed by all humanity
Worshipped and cherished;
Romantically idealized.

Even unreciprocated love had her charms;
Ensconced in the warmth of loving freely.
Giving only, never receiving, never wanting
Celebrating the thrill of loving, for the sake of love.

Love was divine then;
No earthly stains marred her purity
Love was Christ the Lamb-
Sacrificed that the world may engender
Infinite red roses in all their glory,
To fill the world with love.

Where is The Gentle Shower of Love?

Where is the gentle shower of love -
That leaves the psyche, glowing and shimmering?
Like the summer shower refreshing
The hot dusty earth,
Washing clean the blooms and tendrils,
Leaving behind the glittering, refreshing greenery.

The parched psyche thirsty for love,
Yearns nostalgically for the golden days
Of youthful love; of eternal spring;
When everything was a cause for spontaneous joy.

But now life yawns like a chasm,
Devoid of vitalizing showers.
Decayed bones and fossils of dead love-
Grin, scorning the foolish psyche's,
Desire to regain the bliss of love.

Did I Tell You?

Did I tell you
The moment I saw you
My heart missing a beat
Sank to the pit of my being
Painting me blue and pink?

Did I tell you
How my heart was whispering
Your name with every beat
How I yearned for your nearness
While pretending that you did not exist?

Did I tell you
Even as I watched someone else
My inner eyes were on you
Capturing stills of your movements
To be encased in the album of my heart?

Did I tell you
When you called my name
Ever so softly like the whisper
Of the falling leaves
My heart flew out to you?

Did I tell you
I trapped it
And caged it securely
For no one to spy it
In my naked eyes?

Did I tell you
That I dare not look at you.
For you would glimpse the truth
I never wanted to share with any one
Not even with you?

Did I tell you
That I smiled and smiled
While all the while my ego
Urged me to run away
So that I would save my self respect?

Yes, did I tell you
While acting out my meagre role
I was running inside wildly
Searching for nooks and crannies
To hide and lick my bleeding heart?

Did I tell you?
It was to save the last
Vestige of womanly dignity
Before being stoned to death
By the eyes of self-styled Puritans?

Did I tell you
That I loved you -
A love doomed to death
Like a still-born babe
In the womb?

No, I couldn't tell you.
They are the primitive urges
Of the wild self residing in me
Trapped within my conscious self
Leading a custom-bound conventional life.

But let me tell you now
My love, Phoenix-like,
Resurrecting in a friendship perennial -
Is watered by unconditional love,
And sustained by the Almighty sun.

Butterfly

Your passionate love
Gives wings to my soul
To land in a world sublime –
An idealized Utopia!
Where loving vibes of friendship,
Calm, soothe, inspire and protect;
Screening me from all emotional
Onslaughts of the world.

The friendly love and sustenance
Make me flit out - a butterfly,
Fresh from its cocoon, to enjoy
And perceive the world
With sharpened vision
Of love and happiness.

Ache

Beaming sun,
Playing waves,
Dancing schooner,
Preening seagull,
Walloping dolphin -
Amidst the roar of silence
Environed by vast emptiness
Where the sea and the sky meet
At the distant horizon
An awe inspiring grandeur!
Yet for the one on the deck
An unutterable ache
An inexpressible longing for the shore
To be enfolded in his beloved's arms

Hurt

The hurt flower droops
Until the pale petals
Fall one by one
Like tears unnoticed
To mingle with soil-
The very source of its life.

But a distressed heart
Droops awhile,
Learns to shed
Desires, dreams, illusions-
Falling petals;
In recesses deep in the heart
And secretes detachment-
Armour to protect
From the random arrows flung
On the battle ground of survival.

shards

How easy it is!
To shrug of people
Who bared their heart to you?

The pain intolerable,
Leaves behind a fragmented self.
But ego repairs and reinstates
The broken shards.

And like the phoenix
The wounded self rises
From the ashes of burnt friendship.

Patching Up

My heart rend –with tiny, tiny, tears.
Have become holes too big for patching up.
The small ones-patched up neatly on time, flourish.
But the bigger ones have left scars
Too thick to hide.
Appearing ugly and painful to sight-
A constant reminder of the bitter agony
I suffered in the name of friendship.

Prop

Friendship, a prop of life
Who can live without it?
Even the meanest heart
Yearns like the sunflower
For the friendly warmth to bloom;
And share happiness,
Hopes and miseries,
Begotten in the journey of life.

Where can one hoard
Secret loves,
Suppressed yearnings,
Untold miseries
And unspoken desires,
If not in a friend's heart?

Tiny World

Little round eyes rolling,
Tiny hands and legs beating in the air,
Smiling with your toothless gum,
You steal the onlooker's heart.
This charm of winning,
Everyone's affection and love,
Wanes away, as you stand on your feet
Asserting your tiny world of independence.

My Child

With laughing eyes, pouting lips, and a lanky body
A doe, you came nuzzling into my heart
Making me your willing slave.
When sick and fretful,
My heart aches for you -
Longing to see your naughty self,
Wondering-when your drooping eyes,
Would shine with joy and laughter,
And when you would rush about
Amma-ing a thousand times.

Camaraderie

Two piggy tails bobbing,
Shining black eyes laughing,
Weaving funny anecdotes,
You enthrall your 'Acha'
With your childish prater.

Listening patiently,
He supplements with creations similar,
Leading to unrestrained laughter and joy.

I– a silent spectator
Enjoyed the camaraderie
Between father and daughter
Denied to me as a child.

A Mother's Day

The day dawns with a long list-
Of things to be done
Before the sun is up.
The hustle and bustle of routine life-
Begun at four in the morning,
Stretches long-
Reducing one to an automaton.
Cooking, cleaning, packing lunch boxes,
Finally off to work.

If the day turns to be frictionless
It's a pleasure.
But a sour day drains you,
Reducing your job to drudgery.

Back home drained and lethargic
The sight of tired hungry mouths,
Back from school, waiting patiently,
For your arrival,
Kindles fresh energy -
For another round of automatic -
Cooking, feeding, helping with homework,
And lulling them to sleep.

Finally the much awaited private minutes,
Beside the loved one-
Sharing problems, and jokes.
But often these too are stained
By flaring disagreements,
Quickly smothered
By fatigue and sleep-a blessing.

New Nest

Dewy-eyed dawn, twittering songsters,
Eagerly awaiting the golden streaks
To lighten up the world
For the early worms to catch.

In a tiny nest, the she-bird's pride-
Geared up for her first flight,
With mounting excitement.
Wings gathering balance,
The little one circled in the air
With swan like grace
Under the watchful eyes
Of the adoring pair.

The he-bird singing hymns,
Heralding the sun, flew mirthfully,
Cheering the little one, inspiring her to fly
Higher and higher, to race with the wind.

Oblivious of the sorrowful joy, colonizing
The mother-mind; tenderly visualizing
The young one, soon in a nest of her own
Chosen by her beloved for a new life.

Waiting

My ears strain
To catch your footfall
So gentle, so soft, so stealthy
Like the fall of autumn leaves.

Sitting all alone
Doing this, doing that
Driving away apprehensions
Summoned by your delay
Slowly occupying my spirit
Like roosters settling for the night.

Once, my children kept me company.
But now all alone in the big house
I strain, keeping still to capture
Your gentle footfall, on the gravel.

Eve

The bitter agony-
The result of eating
The forbidden fruit
Was it so killing then?
Is it the curse on Eve?
Generation after generation
Such a fruit be tasted
And suffering unwanted, invited?
Can never an Eve
Overcome the forbidden temptation?
Should she always fall?
And eat its consequence?

A Wild Terrain

A world unto herself–
Yielding at each exploration,
Some clue or the other.
But always a wild terrain,
Surprising you at every turn.

An island,
Never revealing completely to anyone,
Though some claim to know her.
Unpredictable–
From the days of Eve
A mystery, unraveled by none –
Yet tantalizing to men.

Lamp

Waiting, waiting for you-
I forgot to light
The lamp of my life-
To give it oil,
To trim it,
To clean the glass.

So as a lamp uncared for;
With smoke covered glass,
My life spent,
The light within,
Never allowed –
To shine brightly;
Day and night-
A terrible waste,
Died an unnatural death-
Slowly waning away-
Another unfortunate Echo.

The Uncanny Singer

Your plaintive sweet notes
Kurni... Kurni... Kurni...
Pierce the atmosphere
With an uncanny premonition,
Sending shudders through my soul
Chilling my being to the bones.

For, you had sensed that awesome presence,
Prowling and stalking in my neighbourhood.
Frightened I wait.
The question - who next?
Tormenting my mind
Until I hear
The nerve breaking announcement
Of someone's departure
To Lethe's shore.

Dream Child

The cold hands of death swept you away.
But you still remain-a part of my being
My very own.

You crept into my heart without my knowledge,
Now I realize, how much you meant to me;
Though not my own.

Your sudden departure - creating a void,
Made me realize-that no one can fill it;.
Unless it is you.

You will live, a shining memory
Till my last breath is gone-
A dream child, I never had.

Corina

Corina my little flower,
Bloomed for a while.
A tiny bud,
Destroyed by the onslaught of rain,
Left me tear-drenched to suffer.

Shattered, I longed for Death.
And he stalked me, a willing slave.
Embracing me in his icy cold grip,
Squeezing my heart and soul,
To comply with him
For the last journey.

But Life cast her hook on me-
To pull me out of his vicious grip,
She enticed me with vignettes
Of my loving family
I ruthlessly planned to leave behind.

Torn between the two,
My will slackened
Life tightened her iron grip
And I was gently wafted
To the world of living.

Dimpled Angel

If you were here, my bud
You could have blossomed
Into a flower so beautiful
A luminous star of attraction!

Spreading the fragrance
Of love and warmth -
Sixteen summers like a day
Have passed, and I see
Your transformation
From a cherubim
To a dimpled Angel.

In your heavenly, sublime home
You watch, pray, plead
And meditate to God,
For your bereaved earthlings
Even now tear drenched,
In your memory.

Bereft

Burning pyre,
Bereft wife
Bewildered children
Agonized hearts
Dancing in pain
Yet waiting, wondering
Numb minds preparing
For tragedies
Not greater than this.

Agony

On an inky black night,
The moon, tear-stained, hid her face
Among the dark manes of the cloudy sky;
Nonchalant stars played hide and seek;
You - came riding the night wind
Slicing the silence of the night
And my mind with shrill,
Sharp, agonized hoots, pulsating
Urgency in the flowing notes.

Adrift in the ocean
Of the subconscious mind,
Pursuing a dream of an elusive kind,
I listened to your soul-rending hoots
Searching for reasons
For such anguished notes.

"Did his beloved leave him for another?
Was the vision of lonely years,
Yawning ahead troubling him?
Did the fledglings' plight worry him?
Was he betrayed by his best friend?
Was he irked by his kins' injustices?
Was he in a state of paralyzing indecision?
Or was he just overwhelmed
By the struggle to survive in a world,
Not always friendly?"

Twisting and turning I tried to gauge
Your sorrow, and find a reason.
But could only throb with your agony
That dreary night, until the arrival of Aurora.

Temptation

How cold the climate!
As cold as the icy fingers of Death,
Wringing and squeezing my heart.
Pain trickled drop by drop,
Creating a pool at the bottom
Of my being,
Slowly swelling into a lake
Drowning me in its vicious depth.

And for a weak moment, I visualized
An edenic possibility -
A perfect relief - for all pains.
A welcome solution – to all problems.
Knowing it is sinful,
The thirst to drink,
From the sweet cup of oblivion-
Was very enticing.

Zombie

When the mind is numb and blue,
Phantoms surround me.
Their masquerades and parades-
Senseless pantomimes.
I move about a zombie,
Welcoming sleep which assails me,
To whisk me to his kingdom of peace.

Lonely Plight

You came into my open veranda
And perched on the hook jutting out.
Glimpsing your ruffled feathers
I bade you goodnight silently
Moving away without disturbing you.

But the next twilight I saw you
Silently gliding in and settling
Comfortably for the night.
In the twilights that followed
You were a familiar sight for me.

Your sleek handsomeness
Your self-possession,
Your assured flight
And encroachment
Upon my privacy,
Irritated me.
This corner,
The lonely twilights
Were mine alone.

Your silent, cocksure presence
Disturbed my serenity.
I tolerated you for a week.
I didn't want my loneliness reinforced
With your solitary presence.

The next morning, I removed the hook
Now sure, you will find a perch elsewhere
Or fly back to your own nest, where
She waited with her fledglings for you,
And I could forget your lonely plight.

When the Birds Sing

When the golden sunbeams
Snake through the morning mist,
When the tender breeze kisses the flowers,
Awakening them to bloom and dance;
When the rabbits stray out to graze,
When the farmers hurry out to their fields,
When the fishermen hasten to their oars,
When the whole world bathed
In morning splendour glistens,
She alone crippled by her heart,
Was confined to her bed bemoaning,
The loss of morning glories.

Taj Mahal

Trapped within the four walls,
Tethered to an oxygen cylinder
Yearning for warmth and sunshine.
Striving to protect a heart so weak,
From the chilly interior
Of a haven, beautiful
You lived
A death in life.

A trapped bird in a cage;
Deprived of companionship
Always giving, never complaining,
A wraith-like figure, painful to encounter.

Yet you waited optimistically,
Believing firmly,
"There is a season for everything"
Even for death.

Black Knight

When the Black Knight
Dressed in splendour,
Came knocking at my door,
I said to him, "I have two fledglings
One hardly four and the other six,
Allow me to tend to their needs."
He left without a murmur.

I wondered why!
But I turned back to life
Enjoying the minutiae of living -
Caring for my loved ones
I saw their wings sprout,
Fourteen summers passed by.

Not a day passed,
Without thanks-giving to my God,
For the reprieve he had given me.
Soon my daughter found a new nest,
My apprehensions about her vanished.
But my younger one's wings
Had hardly any strength,
To survive the gales and storms
That might take him,
So I kept my fingers crossed.

But one evening, most unexpectedly
The Black Knight came riding, riding.
I sensed him from far, for my body
Curiously enough was preparing itself.
To free my soul to its eternal home.
I knew for certain he would not wait
Nor let me be for some more time.
Yet when he reached my door step
I parried with him for one more day.
Sure enough, pity assailed him
He left without a word.

But I knew deep inside
He would come
For me the next day.
And my frail heart
Like a caged bird fluttered
Conscious of the time to fly away.
But I wanted to see the sun,
And people amidst their daily chores
I yearned to be out in the midst of life
Just this once, with my beloved
A last ride together!

Yes, I must get out of this room,
This house, this red, prison.
Maybe God understood
My intense desire.
My friend's unexpected visit
Triggered my desire.
She promised to take me out,
But where? Yet out we went -
To the hospital for a check up.

It was a great day for me.
Flanked by my beloved
And my friend we drove away.
I enjoyed the golden sun,
Peeping through the mighty trees,
The sight of hurrying people,
And rushing life mesmerized me.

The doctor aghast
Admitted me in a room
Where the windows
Opened to the entrance.
I thrilled at the sights I saw.

For the past two years,
Too sick to move about
I had seen only my backyard
And my neighbour's shut windows.
Starved of company, I faded.

Children in search of new pastures,
My beloved busy making money,
None had time for me.
Even my friends kept away
Fearing that their visits would strain
My frail heart and worsen my illness.
No one spied the change
Their presence wrought on me -
Turning rosy and pink, blooming
Blood rushing back to my face,
Erasing the bluish pallor of death.
They never knew my yearnings -
To be in the midst of loved ones.

Passing days sucked me
Into the vortex of despair.
All the loneliness building up
In the red walls of my prison
Made me long for him.
And he came faithfully
And gave me one more day
To enjoy myself.

It was a day of picnic for me!
Surrounded by my loved ones,
The apple, I munched
Tasted like ambrosia.
I talked ceaselessly
Ignoring the tension
Mounting, in their eyes
It was a day of celebration.

Tomorrow I will be no more.
So let me talk my maximum
I talked, I laughed,
I teased my friends,

I pulled their legs,
Oh! It was fun.

The consternation they tried to hide
Made me vicious and I made sly remarks
And barbed digs at my relatives.
But they gracefully ignored them
Their discomfort made me
All the more exuberant,
I talked on ceaselessly
Giving them little chance to speak.

My beloved -
He never left my side
Tending to my needs
Like a slave dutiful
I was overjoyed - at least today
I will have him by my side
He was always slithery as an eel
Slipping away on slightest pretexts.
But today I had really hooked him
I had tied him to my petticoat string.
By evening I was discharged.
My relatives and friends visited me.
And I was totally tired.
I had to prepare for my journey.
Before that I had to finish
Two more tasks -
Bid adieu to my sister,
And my children.

I had completed all the other tasks
I had given away all my best clothes
And all my cherished items
To people who would use them.
I looked forward to my two phone calls.

As I rode home
I feasted on the passing scenes,
And thirstily drank them in.
My last ride!

At home I called my sis
Speaking to her for an hour,
I bade her farewell implicitly,
But her mind wouldn't accept it.
I told her how tired
And fed up I was, protecting
My heart, for survival.
How I had become a burden to everyone,
I then bade her good night and good bye
Time was running out on me.

I called my children,
I couldn't get them.
My heart throbbed painfully
For my children's presence.
I realized I had to go
Without bidding them adieu.

I heard the sound of hooves
Advancing, as my Black Knight
Came galloping from the South.
Once I had conceived of him,
As a grim relentless being.
But experience had proven him
To be kind and merciful.
He had given me fourteen long years,
And one more day
What more can I ask of him
I was tired.

I wanted to sleep
I had no one to care for now.
Even before he reached my door
My soul flew out to him
Cradling it in his arms tenderly
He swung his horse towards eternity.

Aria

Strains of a once familiar song,
Lapping on the shores of my memory.
Tantalized and teased me to pursue
Its' haunting; yet, evading, elusive lines.

In hot pursuit I crashed through -
The labyrinthine maze of my mind,
Stacked high with neatly packed caskets
Of variegated experiences of my life.

In varied colors and shapes,
The gazing memory caskets mocked me.
For, in the haste of living I had forgotten
To label them neatly for future reference.

The glazed, look of the unlabelled caskets,
Unnerved me; with their still, icy silence.
I had forgotten the content of most of them;
An urge to open and reminisce mastered me.

I deliberately ignored that wanton desire.
My soul's undivided aim- to trace the source
Of that familiar song, haunting me relentlessly,
Coerced my mind; to reveal the recurring melody.

The intense quest of my soul seared my being
Vibrating with the agonizingly mounting tempo-
The reverberating echoes of the haunting notes.
In a blue flash unveiled YOU - in my inner eyes.

Like a roaring wave from an alien shore,
The Lydian measure permeated my being
The aria celebrating our idyllic friendship,
For a brief span of ten years.

The recaptured song, from the sea of oblivion-
Created by the "sick hurry, and fret of living";
Flooded and environed my being - memories,
Fluttering like homing pigeons.

Our friendship transcended the earthly barriers,
As if we had been friends for eons, our shared
Thoughts; feelings; attitudes; experiences;
Identical visions of life strengthened our bond.

Yet you lived in a plain sublime;
Your faith and absolute trust in God,
Made you a source of inspiration,
To all, who connected with you.

A unique incarnation of love-You
Accepted, forgave and patiently bore-
The undeserving yoke in your life-
A real model of human virtues.

Oft, I had enjoyed your care and concern;
Your warm presence and letters of consolation,
Had often restored my bruised and injured soul,
Wafting me to serene shores of happiness.

You had bowed helplessly to your fate,
When the relentless Reaper brought to naught-
Your hard won spiritual and earthly honours,
Destroying forever your intense desire to live.

Unreconciled to the reality of loss, I see you
In starched sari, an arm-load of books,
Hurrying to classes, your bespectacled eyes
Smiling greetings to friends and students.

I see you immersed in post-doctoral studies,
Guiding your students, or bustling about
Attending to never ending womanly chores
As wife, daughter-in-law, friend and teacher.

All these images instill in me a fond hope-
The hope of meeting you soon...as though
I need only to put aside my daily chores
And make a surprise visit as in yester years.

Spark

Was there no positive
Spark, a speck, a flicker,
To keep you going my child?
Didn't the evergreen classics
You read and the great souls
You communicated with
Provide a spark to keep
You going my child?

Uncared-for, unloved, a vagabond -
Exposed to the sinister side of life,
What led you to the freakish cruelty?
An abused being, never enjoying
The warmth of affection, what else
Could his child brain teach him?
A hermit – you crawled into yourself;
Dwelling in the dark subconscious.
Your arrival in the juvenile home
Was a blessing, but short-lived.
Yet you left a glow behind
For millions of little ones like you
Exposed to the seamier side
Of this wide world.

No loving hands to guide them,
Or stroke them or pat them
With understanding;
No loving lips to appreciate them,
To encourage them;
No one to help them discern.
The black and the white -
So cursed to live in shades of grey -
Confused, bewildered.
All that a child needs for blossoming,
Denied and nipped off in the bud!

But— you, my child,
Had a chance of coming back -
A saviour brought you
Back to normal life
Building up your inner strengths,
Identifying your taste for reading,
Opening, a new world of books.
Swimming up the dark stream
Of sub-conscious you reached
A new shore - the world of letters -
A fish, enjoying the fresh water.

Thriving in the new knowledge
Of the Koran and the Bhagavad Gita,
Basheer and MT were your favourites,
APJ's books you perused avidly,
Kadamanitta's poetry rejuvenated you,
"Kozhi" your favourite, you recited
With a flourish to enthralled listeners;
A talented singer, a wizard with colours -
Yes, you came back to life!

Within a short span,
A thousand and more books
You perused. But all brought to naught!
The dark shadows of two-faced life
Stalked you.

No soul could stop you, child,
From destroying yourself.
No spirit was there
To extend a loving hand,
To pull you out of that slushy mire
That swallowed you up.

Yet you will remain a spark,
A guiding spirit,
To children like you -
A shining light to lead them,
Through the world of letters
To a better world.

Elizabeth

A rebirth for me this life,
A painful gift
Without mother or father.

Locked in parental embrace,
We never heard the roar of the waves
Nor, felt the tremors of the earth.

Death came to us in sleep;
Leaving me behind,
To face the tribulations of rebirth.

Me, a miracle for the rescuers,
Retrieved from the womb of the earth
After seventy-two hours.

Ensconced by the frigid bodies
My parents left behind,
While traveling Lethe wards.

Aylan Kurdi

Aylan Kurdi, my child
You have invaded my being;
I shall never close my eyes again
Without seeing you vividly
In your red shirt and blue trousers
And your brown shoes intact -
(A combo enhancing your chubby looks -
A regular baby Bimbo
Stealing everyone's heart).
Lying face down on the sand
Etched clearly in my mind.

The first glimpse I had of you,
I surmised you were playing.
But something unnatural in the pose,
Made me scroll back for a closer look -
And the shock of comprehension
Made me tremor with agony,
Leaving behind a dull ache.

Oh Aylan! your inert body
In red and blue pierced my heart,
Mocking me in my helpless, uselessness.

Oh Aylan! how callous we have become!
Ensconced in our personal lives
We close our eyes to the suffering around.

Oh Aylan! when will we wake up
To the realization – *lokame tharavaadu?*
That we have space to live as one big family.

Oh Aylan! I lash myself
Every time I see a red and blue combo -
A symbol of the world's and mine callosity.

Game of Survival

Born to love and live!
Yet loving and living
Reduced to art of manipulation.
Success was skill pushing
The naïve and the innocent
Into depths unfathomed.
Where the cruellest
Game of survival
Is played relentlessly.

To Irom Shormila

Your sacrifice to redeem a people
Surviving persecution fills me with pride
To be part of the same humanity.

Yet it shames me – a passive witness
To your torture of body and soul
For a cause so noble.

Separated by geographical distance
I cling on to your invisible hand
Empathizing with your struggle.

A smouldering volcano,
Strengthening you,
Expressing my solidarity -

So that our sisters and brothers
Soon taste the air of freedom
And live without fear.

To Live Freely

What can I do for my people?
Greatest love in the world-
Sacrificing your life for your friend.

This is my way of showing love!
Dying inch by inch to change stone hearts.
What else can a frail creature like me do?

This, I see as my destiny!
Someone will see me!
Someone will hear me!

After twenty-eight dormant years
I live vibrantly now
For a mute people.

Ten wintry years - yellow leaves
Falling silently,
Wrought no changes.

I brushed not my teeth
In fear that a drop of water
Be swallowed to defeat the cause.

My body and soul dedicated
To ensure freedom for my people
To fearlessly survive the iron rod of the oppressor.

Hope

Hope springs up-
A bubble in the stream of life
Buoyantly floating a while,
But bursting at slight pricks,
Of rushing debris of life's spate.

But, way down the life stream,
It bobs up among the frothy ripples,
To dance jubilantly down the stream.

So goes the bubble of hope,
Sustaining the game of life
Until, the last round is played.

Onam

Onam approaching
Air filled with gaiety,
The festive spirit throbbing,
Infusing happiness everywhere.

But bewildered self,
Yearning for answer
To a question
Yet un-answered.

Is the heart prepared
To receive the greatest of givers,
Pushed to 'pathal'
By the relentless Gods?

The Crown of Creation

I looked up at the sky-
The grandeur of the new day,
Thrilled my veins.

I peeped down into the valley-
Of gay, dancing flowers unfurling,
Celebrating another dawn.

I perceived the winged beings,
Fluttering and twittering abundantly,
Keeping rhythm to natures' music.

I observed the four legged creatures,
Hurrying and scampering to fulfill,
Infinite desires of their instinct.

I spied the white currents whirl
Foaming and frothing as they swirl,
Riding the high seas untethered.

I looked at the crown of creations
They alone appeared flurried and harried–
By desires infinite.

Elves and Goblins

Dreams - elves or goblins
Jauntily, stealthily, pervading
Mind's subconscious bowers
To lay siege to the sleeping mind -
A stage for dreams -
Enacted by elves and goblins,
Depending on the themes chosen
To unravel life's mysteries.

Comedy, romance, tragicomedy,
Revenge, horror and realistic dreams –
A rich repertoire! All staged
Without prior notice.
The lone spectator - the conscious mind
Sits agape as the uncanny spirits take the stage
Elves soothe, wafting the spectator to havens
Of happy interludes, luck and prosperity.

And the prancing goblins
Representing themes of horror
Rock the human body
Sending tremors of trepidations
Or suffocating the dreamer
To emerge struggling for breath
As if forcibly ducked in fathomless water
Reducing them to shivering jelly.

For me dreams are elves
With occasional goblins sneaking through
Guiding me, leading me to realms strange
Beyond ordinary ken; to revel
In happiness, a light from the inner spirit
Aiding me to pick my way through paths
Untrodden filled with thorns and jagged stones
To reach my destination intact.

Traitorous Thoughts

Traitorous thoughts with their octopus grip
Playing with emotion's unpardonable, sinful,
Pervade my being triumphantly;
Creating havoc in my mind,
Trying to escape its grim grip.

They come creeping into my mind
Even when the doors are locked -
Like the invisible gold dust
That streamed into the castle
And impregnated Danae.

The stealthy colonizers settle snugly.
My vain attempts to shove them out
Only vitalizes them to stubbornly
Spread roots in my heart
And inhabit there.

Chaotic Thoughts

Shattered pieces of crystals
Each a world unto itself
Reflecting the reality
In dimensions distorted
To a mind in frenzy
Driven by chaotic
Gales of thoughts.

Oh! take away this cup of wine,
Bitter sweet in its intensity
So may I survive yet another day
In joy, oblivious to the storm
Raging in my heart.

Jekyll and Hyde

Mind – a torturing rack,
Guilt- laden heart,
Love - reduced to lust,
Jekyll writhes in agony,
Hyde triumphantly proceeds,
Will reduced to a shivering jelly,
Helplessly watches the march of
Wanton desire towards fulfillment.

A Feathery Thing

My heart –a feathery thing,
Longs to fly away.
From the torments of the flesh
And perch on Fancy's wings
A mad fling to come back
Calm and restored
To take up the heavy reins of life.

A Ride on Fancy's Wings

Nestling down in an arm chair
At moth hour reading a book;
Slipping into a trance I wandered.
Fancy drew me to spy a quaint machine
Intricately designed with a seat;
Alice like I entered the automaton
Heedlessly hitting a switch, it took off.

Flying on the wings of Time
Swishing past, verdurous Earth
The eonator headed a wormhole.
Its sinister darkness sent
Ripples of fear down my spine
But within seconds I was out;
I arrived in a mystic land of splendour
Rivers and streams, hillocks and mountains;
A land of strange animals and alien people.

Mastering control of the machine
I landed in a grove. My roving eyes
Alighted on a mysterious creature.
My eyes feasted on its singular beauty.
Its silvery horn adorning its forehead,
Gleamed bright as it nimbly trotted
On its cloven hooves; its luminous mane
Thick and long, glittered gold in the sun,
The lion tail rustled silvery stream.

Hiding behind the trees in the woody haven,
Bedecked with multi-hued flowers infinite,
I pursued the animal as it ambled along
Nibbling softly the grass, at times assessing
The sylvan environs, it paused in a glade open,
A glinting crystal pond reflected the azure sky
And the florid trees mirrored a garden enticing.

The air was filled with music enchanting;
Listening mesmerized, my gaze fell upon
An ethereal being; gliding over the grass,
Almost human except for her golden wings
Clad in a gossamer gown, exquisitely spun,
Embellished delicately with roses red.
She touched its silvery horn, an alluring sight
As the animal knelt adoringly at her feet.
A unicorn, I realized as she swung on
To its back and galloped away.

The galloping sound receded
And the tick-tock of the clock
Diffused my being to wakefulness
Drenching me with disappointment –
For losing grip of a strange universe
Far away from human ken.

Drying Spring

The pain of being a woman in her late forties
A drying spring, battling to ooze out,
To cling on to life
With odds heavily ranged against her.

Creaking bones,
Stiff joints on strike,
Invasion of cancerous cells,
Fettered to oxygen cylinder for breath,
Yet, striving dauntlessly
To execute
The daily chores of life.
Playing the multiple roles,
Of being a woman.

The body, a rusting machine plaguing the mind
With preying thoughts ferocious and relentless
Ruthlessly driving it to retreat
Into caverns of sub consciousness,
To hide from the jitters and the pity of the world,
To lick the wounds to heal, and to retrieve
The instinctive womanish nature for survival.

And then to march out, suitably
armed and encounter,
The world unflinching, holding on
To the outstretched arms of the inner grace
Once lost, but now found.

The Trapped Bird

The night wrapped its shroud,
Hiding everything under its folds.
She listened to the gentle snores
Of her beloved and her child.
But her heart alone -
A trapped bird, fluttered
From thought to thought.

The reality, the truth of being a woman
Stereotypical images of womanhood -
Abject beings, self-effacing doormats,
Shaped by patriarchal hegemony
An angel of the house,
A perfect woman
Haunted her.

A sudden vision of unlimited horizon
Opened, releasing the trapped bird
To fly to heights unknown.

Visibility

Woman
Just body and womb?
A disturbing question!
Her dreams? -
To live gloriously,
Victoriously, with self dignity
Standing erect and tall,
United, powerful, diligent,
Rising above physical abuse and violence,
Transcending mutilation Philomela like,
Singing songs of fulfillment,
Weaving stories of truth
Overcoming barriers – linguistic,
Economic, political and cultural
Destroying invisibility.

Wild Woman

She surfaced
Through myriads
Of materialistic layers
Overpowering and taming the self –
Ensconced in mores and traditions.
A butterfly - beautiful and natural
A life force, free, unhampered
A spirit of attunement,
Leading to pathways strange
Hitherto submerged and hidden.

Trusting her heart, listening
To the small guiding voice inside -
Primitive, yet authentic and true to self
Doing what gives joy - laughing, crying,
Waltzing, bawling, sniffing,
Gnarling, scratching, loving,
Running free, snoozing
The female soul; scintillating,
Sagacious, intuitive-
The source of feminine endurance.

Perennial Inspiration

A source of perennial inspiration
You make me bloom with joy
For being born in your blessed womb.
Have I ever told you dear Amma?
Like the moon influenced sea
Thoughts about you
Bring out the best in me.

Rocking Lap

You rocked me on your lap
Satiating me with stories infinite
Now, when I think of you *Paattie*
The characters parade before me -
The foolish tortoise, the cunning fox,
The credulous crow, the mischievous girl,
The friendly stork, the stupid rabbit -
A world of fantasy and make believe.
Often when I am miserably lonely
I imagine sitting near you,
Listening to world-wise stories,
Feeling rejuvenated, I resume my life.

Paattie
(Granny)

I see you –
Face lined with wrinkles,
Of living and suffering
Double loss-of husband and son
A cruel stroke of the Reaper,
Reduced you to a human vegetable.

Living for no one-
Not even for yourself.
Fed and clothed and led by hand
A child; needing constant attention.
Spending your time, talking
To yourself as in a trance-
Reminiscing your happy days,
None could draw you out of your past.

But children were your weakness –
Your faded eyes full of love,
Twinkled with mirth
At our childish pranks.

I found solace in your company –
Your betel red lips
Ever ready to comfort me,
Smoothened my ruffled emotions,
With gentle words.

You listened to my childish woes
And filled me with confidence,
I thrived on your infinite fund of stories –
And rode on fancy's wings.

Now – oft tossed by the storm of life
Memories of those days -
Serve as an oasis for my tired mind
To roost, and be re-energized.

You and I

The face-
A faded rose.
The eyes,
Two sunken wells –
Drowning thoughts
Too deep for expression.

You –
Engrossed in purchasing
Mechanically,
The short list of groceries.

I –
Spied you in the shop.
My heart went out to you,
Longing to share your sorrows,
Etched vividly on your wrinkles.

But my selfish duties,
Drew me away.
Your face
I tucked,
Into the corner of my mind.
To remind me of people like you.
Suffering from neglect and loneliness.

Black Beaded Chain

Busy buying toys for my grandson
Outside Mother Mary's Church,
I hardly noticed her.
But, I heard her request
To my surprised partner -
"Please, give me ten rupees".

I turned round,
A fair, beautiful, wrinkled face,
Well attired,
In *mundu* and *kavany* -
A face that pierced my heart,
The eyes innocent; yet pleading.

Extending a ten rupee note,
I smiled at her.
She took it, eyes brimming
Kissed my hands; overwhelmed,
Tears sped down my cheeks,
Unabashed, unchecked.
I hugged and kissed her.
Onlookers - my family
And the shopkeeper.

Handing twenty rupees
To the shop keeper
She waited; an expectant child
"Okay, take it", he gave her -
A small brown packet.
She extended it to me.

It contained a black-beaded chain!
Her excitement at the purchase
Rippled through her to me, I spied
A small girl with her precious find.
"Will you put it around my neck?"
"Sure", I said, tears streaming down

Yet beaming eyes,
An unexpected privilege.
"Kollaamo?" *"Ummm"*,
I nodded.
She hugged me.
"You are my daughter, I have only sons,
You have made me happy,
I shall pray for you my child."

She left me.
I stood in a trance
My Mother?
Mother Mary?
An aura of beatitude
Light hearted,
I turned around to my family
Standing amazed and bewildered.

The First Christmas Card

I remember the day
A card, yellowed and crisp,
Yet cherished and protected –
In a box lined with red velvet
Was shown to me.

Bedimmed eyes reflecting shyness
Excitement in her demureness,
A teenager bubbling to reveal a secret
She whispered softly, drawing me closer
"I have not shown this to anyone,
But you are special, you understand."

Swallowing my surging tears
Wrought by the unexpected compliment
I stood holding tightly my breath,
Lest I disturb her dreamy meanderings
Into bygone days of life and love.

I watched her age-worn hands
Tenderly extract the card,
To reveal within an enchanting bower
Splendidly adorned with greenery
And flitting love birds, a handsome
Artist engrossed in painting
A portrait of his beloved.

I spied the heart of the giver
In that cherished, first Christmas card.

Nature's Magic Spell

Down in the glade
Near the crystal clear pond
Shining Sapphire in the sunlight
Spying on the silvery fishes,
Playful snakes and watchful herons
I sat ensconced
In nature's magic spell.

Notes of Joy

The tiny bird in the lawn,
Making his musical concert,
Thrilled me with his inner joy,
Proclaimed to the world-
Through peals and peals of melody.

Spontaneous, unrestrained
The notes of sheer ecstasy –
Pierced my heart, drawing me out
To listen to the song of joy.
Wondering what thrilling emotion
Inspired this black and white feathery singer -
To sing his heart rending song,
Making me tingle with every note?

Little Mynah

Little mynah on the palm leaf
Nodding head vigorously,
Frantically twittered
To attract the attention
Of his sweetie near by.

She-carelessly disregarding
His love call,
Indulged in her task
Of collecting worms.

Minnows

Minnows, playing in the stream,
Conscious of danger-
Lurking behind every sedge and rush
Play on, living in the moment.

Unlike man- worrying and fretting,
What morrow holds for him?
Forgetting to live in the present,
Forsaking the joy and the thrill of living.

The Rill

The rill sparkling in the sun,
Mesmerized me drawing me
To a world of enchantment.

I - a silent observer,
Parched and thirsty for nature's wonders
Drank in the beauty.

Dragon flies darting in and out of the sedges,
Skimming and surfing,
Chasing their lovers.

Fishes flashing their silvery scales;
The water fowls playing hide and seek-
In the coverts of rocks and sedges.

But the most spectacular act was-
The dancing sun beam caressing the stream,
And sweeping her into his golden arms.

Boys and Girls

Tiny flowers blooming
Dressed in yellow,
Purple, blue and pink-
Mischievous little girls
Playing in the wild.

The tender breeze –
Naughty boys
Pulling their hair,
Tearing their ribbons,
Hugging and shoving,
Created havoc among them.

Evening Sky

The fluffy clouded evening sky-
Fascinated me, a child then.
Every evening I watched

The clouds match,
Their strength, against the playful zephyr;
Driving to shape them to his will.

I thrilled, with each identification
I made of the earthly manifestation-
Riding on Fancy's wings.

Even now, caught in time's whirlpool
Bleeding and torn I surface,
To chase the clouds, conquering them-
To ride them to Fancy's abode
To be rejuvenated.

Intimacy

The azure sky,
Streaked with gold -
Golden threads interspersed
In an orange-blue sari.
Made me yearn to drape it
And waltz down the street,
Showing off to my friends
Our intimacy.

Memory

The sea embraces the shore
The rough and gentle waves
Leave painful marks on the shore,
Often carrying away a part of it
To its deep bosom
Maybe to retain the memory
Of the sweet or harsh embrace.

Tree

Branching, sheltering,
Perennial emblem of prayer-
A symbol of love and tolerance.
Giving space to young saplings,
Allowing creepers to intertwine,
Sans caste, creed or position –
To mar their happy relation.

Bound only by universal law-
Live and let live,
Ever conscious of mother earth's bounty.
Sharing generously-
Air, water, sunlight and soil,
Everything needed for its survival.
A prototype of universal love and brotherhood-
A tree is a paradigm for warring humanity.

Love Birds

Engrossed we were in love
Unconscious of the danger
Lurking behind leaves
Yellow and green.

But quick eyes alert and watchful spied
The gliding, glittering creep,
Embodiment of evil,
Plotting to snatch one of us.
Sudden awareness of our vigilance
Made him sheepishly glide away.

The Winged Offenders

The tender flowers that bloom
Are raped by winged offenders
Never dreaming
Their natural acts can kill life.
But this is the way of life
From the very beginning-
One suffering
The other taking for granted.

Earth Mother

"Don't kill the world; she's all we have…"
A haunting melody permeates my soul.
Drilling, excavating, mining, tearing, rending
The womb of mother earth, man thrives.

The quakes, landslides, storms, blood rain-
Her agonized screams and tears for reprieve,
Fall on deaf ears made insensitive
By the roar of materialistic living.

Her agony over the years,
Arouses the "badrakali" in her-
Revengeful and terrible-
To dance her death-dance
To warn the insensitive humans.

Magic in the Air

My autumnal dawns
Unfurling in oppressive stillness;
Stirred nostalgic memories
Of festal mornings.

There was magic in the air once.
I- a child girl
Awoke to Nature's rhapsodies,
Heralding Aurora
Giving wings to my thoughts,
And life to my languidly waking body.

The misty coldness of the fresh dew;
The scent of jasmine pure;
Wafting in through windows ajar,
Driving me to delve deeper
Into the warm bed.

And listen half awake
To the clanging vessel of the milkman
On his early rounds of milking;
To listen to *paattie'* s muffled monologue
Or my *amma's* soft instructions to the maid;
Followed by her morning litanies,
To the floating notes of Suprabhat;
To the early songsters, harbingers of -
Apollo's mighty entourage.

Lure me to roll out of my bed
To run down to the tiny pool,
To drink with my eyes the crystal clear water;
Catching the golden gleam of
the snaking sun beam.
To partake in the joy of the occasional fish
Surfacing for air; or waltz with the water snake
In his serpentine dance.

But now nothing happens.
All recedes as reality rushes in –
And the clock ticks on.
Sadly I toss about.
Where has it all gone?

The herons and the water fowls
Have migrated to marshy fields,
The cuckoos, the swallows, the wagtails,
The magpies and the finches have flown away –
In search of verdurous greens.

No water, no trees, only parched lands,
Marred by edifices of bricks and cement.
No rambling houses,
No cow sheds and hen coops,
No yard with gigantic mango trees,
Jack trees or tamarind trees;
Not even space -
For a swing for a little one!
Only matchbox houses huddling together,
And every village green
Turned to dusty, smoky towns.

The sunken eyes of the parched earth,
Gaping amidst the cement jungle,
Reflected the fear and sorrow gripping my soul
Mourning the death of ceremonious festal dawns.
And, in their despairing, unfathomable depth
I saw mirrored, my own wistfulness-
For the magical symphony heralding Aurora.

What Am I Now?

What am I now? A haven once!
Now a shriveling wasteland.
The oceans, once a blue girdle
Swelling unfathomably
Swallows me, python-like
The azure sky, a diadem
Adorning my head,
Now deprives me
Of life-giving air.

My children, the humans -
Destroy my forests, trees, rivers,
Hills, and vales rebelliously.
The living land - to cement jungle
And garbage pits reduced.

I don't know what I am now!
I am sick with cyclones,
Tremors and fire storms,
Yet the thirst for survival besets me.
Senile, losing control of body and spirit
I wonder! Do my children,
My earthlings, see my struggle?
Will they revive me to survive,
Harmoniously with them?

Wild Furies

Rosy fingered dawn
Dancing on the placid sea,
Enticed the early morning walkers
To the beach,
Children spilled on the shore,
Engaged in enchanting games.
Unsuspecting fisher folk hastened,
Gearing up for the days' fishing.

The half-awake village, groggy-eyed
Embarked on her daily chores.
Far away, in the dark, inky depth
Of the fathomless ocean,
Tethered in stables cavernous,
The wild furies-restive and impatient
Thrashed and lashed the ocean bed

Mother earth rocked and quaked.
The harness broke.
Unleashing the furies to surface-
To race thousand miles per hour,
To wreak vengeance
For their unjust captivity,
On that fatal morn.

The foaming, frothing, ocean-
Million, wild, stampeding horses,
Attacked ferociously, the benign, calm shore.
Gigantic dragon waves
Swallowed land and people;
Satiated, spat out the residue.

Debris of ruined buildings
Uprooted trees,
Mangled vehicles and humans-
Injured, maimed, half alive,
Lifeless bodies
To be ululated.
By the witnesses-
Survivors of natures' holocaust!

To count the onslaught
Of the unbridled Tsunamis
That ravaged their lands,
And snatched away
Their loved ones,
To the under world of dark waters.

The golden glow
Of the unperturbed dusky sun,
Fingered and stroked
Caressingly the protean waves,
Calming and soothing
To lead them away
To be tethered
In the cavernous stables
In the oceans depth.

Placid Pond

The placid pond, still and deep
Environed by flowering trees -
A garden of flowers
In a blue-white setting,
Enjoying the sun and the shade,
Luxuriating in the life it sustained –
The dancing snakes,
The croaking frogs,
The flashing fishes,
The skimming dragonflies,
The chirpers and the hummers
Hovering over the sedges green.

Suddenly a star fell from nowhere
Perturbing the placid water to overflow
Birthing a new stream, in search
Of shallow plains and valleys new.

Where Shall We Go?

The rich paddy fields have disappeared.
Springs, ponds and waterholes are visions
Enthralling us in our sleep.
June's advent makes us flutter;
The excitement mounting
With the advance of monsoon.

The storm and the rain,
And the rising water,
Floating and croaking,
Mating and spawning,
Streams and ponds and puddles,
Soon bubbling with infinite tadpoles.

Future warriors of nature!
Feeding on insects and mosquitoes,
Harmful to nature and man,
Farmers' friends, occasionally hunted,
Never, we grudged our delicious legs,
For, we were aplenty.

But now our wetland usurped,
We sit dismally in waterholes
Shallow, dirty and poisoned
Deprived of food, deprived of water
Chemical fertilizers, pesticides, our bane
We die in hordes, of hunger,
Thirst and poison.

We are now a handful of survivors;
Tired of fighting a vain battle;
Living each day wondering
Where shall we go?

Anguish

A half-dead gigantic tamarind tree,
Standing near a live kiln
Seared my soul whenever I passed it.

The heat rising from the kiln
Killing it day by day.
The side exposed to heat
Singed and seared- russet and grey
The other half, lush and green,
Giving it a freaky look-
A weird tree in some ghostly fantasy.

The agony of the tree - living and dying-
Another illustration
Of the callousness of the humans –
Including me
To nature's denizens,
Made me writhe in shameful anguish.

shaddock

I heard you weep earth-child
As you lay uprooted on your side -
A tragedy wrought by incessant rain
And the earth carved out from your side
For the creation of a basketball court.

I watched you from my window-
Your mute agony lacerated my heart.
I lashed at myself, at my passiveness
But I did nothing, like everyone else,
And waited for the authority to act.

Your fresh leaves and tender shoots
Blooming, in spite of your agony
Reflecting your desire to survive,
Tortured my guilty soul into planting
A shaddock in my yard.

One morning at my window
My shocked eyes captured a still -
Small pieces of logs neatly piled
On a truck and the spot cleared,
Leaving no trace of a tree there.

Lord of the Night

Yellow eyes dilated with fear,
Huddling in the make-shift cage;
Sack and tarpaulin in tatters, to cover,
To protect from the sun's rage,
The sensitive eyes, wistful and sad,
For the dark hide-outs pining,
Yet, the mounting tempo of the mad
Boisterous excitement of spying
You so close, provoked the twin
Golden bulbs, to flash on us the ire,
Out of relentless confinement born,
Helplessly smouldering inside like fire.

King of the night,
Farmers' friend,
Hunter of rodents,
Sentry of the ripened fields,
In the twilight, when the world
To sleep descends,
You come gliding from
Far off woods or meads
Or dilapidated shelters,
Daytime refuge for sleep,
To assume sentry duty,
To watch over our crop,
At bay to keep snakes,
Mice and other rodents
No farmer can get a better prop.

Yet feared and dreaded as an evil one
A bird of ill omen; to Death, a harbinger.
But I secretly loved you - often
A source of curiosity and wonder -
Oft riding on Fancy's wings'
I visualized you as a monster bird -
Built upon the superstitious descriptions
Garnered from the gray-haired villagers
But the pitiable sight - my eyes met -
A bundle of feathers, muddy-white,
On twig legs, sporting yellow eyes,
A rag puppet –
A king fallen to doom
A plight - wrenching my heart
On the human insensitivity
On nature's darlings inflicted.

I ached to gather you in my arms,
To kiss and console you, to let
You fly far away, from human harm
To lick your wounds and heal yourself.
And rally forth the undisputed
Lord of the night.

Shall I Let Her Go?

"Shall I let her go?"
Filled with anguish
I looked around.
"Do away with her,
Females are a curse!"
Looking at the smirking faces
Unclouded with the shadow of sympathy
My eyes caught the unkind gleam,
Echoing the crowd's wish,
In the lone woman's eye.
I turned away to hide my agony
Slowly surging out as a raging anger.

My heart bleeding for her,
I threw the noose around her neck.
The animal trust and love unconditional
I spied in her eyes,
And wagging tail,
Made me squirm inside.
Her bigness gnawed my insides
Like a bird of prey tearing my flesh.
Perspiring I turned to the village crowd
Their blood-thirsty expectancy
Nauseated me.

A Judas, I betrayed her
With the lethal shot.
Whimpering she fell down
Her large eyes fixed on me.
Tears pouring down my cheeks
I hastened away, cursing my life, my job.

"Why is it taking such a long time?"
A disturbing question echoed in my ears.
"She would have delivered
In a day or two."
Some one answered.
Then silence.

Sans Fangs, Sans Teeth

I danced rhythmically
To the swaying *magudi.*
Tired, my torn jaws
Oozing blood and pus
I longed for rest,
Creeping into some hole
Where, in its soothing darkness
I could sleep till my bruised jaws healed,
To resume my life without fangs and teeth.

Then something happened.
A stranger pushing the crowd aside
Strode forward with authority -
I swiped at him with my fangless hood
Only to be caught deftly.
I tried to free myself
Twisting and turning
Between his fingers,
His grip only tightened.

What next?
My heart filled with fear.
I folded my hood,
And held my head far away,
To prevent further hurt
On my swollen jaws;
The stranger released me
And I swiftly coiled
Inside my basket.

But within seconds I felt
Groping hands on my head
He pulled me out and opened my jaws.
The look of empathy I spied in his eyes
Mitigated my fear.
I went limp in his hands,
Sensing instinctively the care
That awaited me.

Washing my wounds, injecting medicine
He gently released me
To the comfort of my basket
Where I coiled tightly to sleep
To forget man-hurt and humiliation.

I woke up two days later
When I felt being lifted.
The same gentle hand
And soothing murmur
Bidding me farewell,
Released me on a leafy surface;
I hesitated only for a moment.

The earthy, woody smell
Assailed me and I slid away
In a lightning flash
In search of a new home
Far away from humans.

Ecstasy

Lips blistered,
Parched and thirsty,
Peeling skin in tatters,
Hair unkempt - Mother Earth -
Watched her little ones struggle
For life-giving water.
Helpless, she raced to escape,
To find succour and relief away
From the agony of her children
Crying of thirst.

The rain came down
First a few random drops -
Gathering speed and momentum;
Driving away the heat, diffusing
The intoxicating scent of the earth,
Bringing out the snakes
To taste the first drops.

The rain came down,
Sheets of opaque glass.
Hiding the ecstasy of mother
Dancing her welcome,
With outstretched arms.
Casting off her tatters.
Drenched and soaked,
Saturated and brimming
With joy and fulfillment
She sank gratefully
Water lapped.

The rain came down
Puddles turned to pools,
Pools over brimmed to streams.
The gurgling of the streams
Merging with the symphony
Of the cicadas, drowned by
The euphoric concert of frogs,
Soothing and comforting, lulled
Mother Earth to sleep
By her satiated children.

Nature at My Doorstep

The black and white robin,
A visitor regular, at my kitchen window,
Piping his sweetest song interspersed with
Signals for food, morning and dusk,
Branded a lazy bird, by my partner,
Thrilled me.
For, doesn't he love me?
Doesn't he come calling for me?
A sign - Nature has adopted me.
The handful of rice I scatter for him,
Makes him cock his head and wait.
I invite him *"Va vanthu sappidu"*
Withdrawing, not to scare him.

Landing gracefully
On my kitchen veranda,
He pecks on the rice daintily,
While I watch with awe and wonder,
Nature at my doorstep.

Extended Family

He comes stealthily with the dawn
Settling down comfortably, his tiny feet astride
The thin branch of the nutmeg tree,
Eyes glued to the kitchen window,
Ears straining to grasp our movements
He waits patiently. If silence greets him
He breaks into shrill chittering
Piercing my ears to roll off my bed.
Prayers forgotten, I run to my kitchen
Straining the rice kept for our wild family
I empty the cupful on his empty platter.
Watching him scramble in excitement
I extend my hand pleadingly inviting him
To feed from my hand. Rushing down
Fear assaults he stops, flicking his tail
He scoots off to his favourite corner.
Bidding him to eat, I hasten to tell
My morning prayers.

There are days I sleep off through his call
Rushing out, I scan the branches
The emptiness sears my soul.
I place his share on the plate and wait hopefully
A dull ache permeating my being
I start my morning chores.
As we settle for breakfast we hear him
I rush to my kitchen
There framed by my window I see him
Daintily eating on one side of the plate
On the other in companionable
silence The one legged crow.
The sight splashes rainbow colours of joy
Brimming eyes full of gratitude
For my extended family
I continue my chores.

Memento

The grey- green *Arayaal* leaf
Pressed between the pages -
A gift of love from nature,
Spurred me on to reminisce.

A perfect evening it was
The crowd was customary
The sylvan retreat, the city's pride
Looked enticing as we strolled in
My daughter clinging on to my hand.

My eyes dancing wantonly
Captured vignettes after vignettes
Young couples, playful children,
Elderly men and women,
Family groups, teenagers,
Squirrels, birds, flowers,
Butterflies and dragon flies;
Nothing I missed of the scenes -
Variegated splendour of life.
Often enthralled, I would stop
Only to be jerked to awareness
By my child's impatient tug.

The path led to my favoured haunt
Beneath the awning shade of the *Arayaal*.
Spying no vacant wooden seats, we stood
Gazing at his symmetrical, graceful, shape,
Kissing the sky in majestic sway,
Tall and straight, branches on all sides,
He was the best of trees I had ever seen
Listening to his joyous whisper
I stood mesmerized.

Suddenly I awoke from the trance
To feel a feathery stroke on my head
Moving gently down my face, my body,
Creating goose bumps as it tickled down
To rest at my feet rooted to the spot.

I spied, in the fading light a leaf –
Perfect and glistening, oozing milk.
Tenderly picking it, I was surprised.
No wanton wind had blown then
To savagely pluck the tender leaf.
And cast it away so brutally.

Unless a gift for me – a wild, mad, guess
Uttered aloud unconsciously,
Quizzing eye of my daughter
Caught me, urging me to whisper –
"A gift of love from the tree, child."
"Love?" her eyes teased blandly,
Tossing her head sprightly
She pulled me along gently.

Bemused, I ambled along
The leaf haunted me in an odd way
Perfectly heart shaped, flawlessly made,
I did not have the heart to throw it away
It clung to me queerly; I took out my dairy
And lovingly placed it between its pages.

The sojourn to maternal home ended.
We reached home; to pick up threads
Of routine life left behind;
The next morning, my spouse
Scanning the news paper
Pointed out a still – a gigantic tree

Uprooted and a requiem for it –
The mighty sentry at the museum portal
A cynosure of every passing eye,
A comfort zone to tired limbs,
Ripped out ruthlessly
By an unpredictable gale,
The previous night.

Stunned, I ran to my desk
Opening the dairy I looked at the leaf
A gift of love to the consigned one!
I felt honoured - a unique memento from Nature.
To be engraved in gold and treasured.

Colours of Eternity

Oft, in the silence of deep thought
Your adorable, omniscient presence
Environ me in colours of eternity.
I get glimpses of your omniscience,
Your cosmic theology.
Secure in such knowledge,
I surge forward arrogantly, vainly.

Forgetting the open jaws
Of the crafty plotter,
Sliding down his slimy interiors,
I reach square number one in no time.
Shaken and contrite, I arduously
Toil up the ladder, watchful and careful
To reach square hundred
And partake in the heavenly joy.

Light

Talking to God eases my pain.
Faith alone pulls me through
The labyrinth of dark thoughts-
One giving way to another.

Trapped in their midst I suffocate.
But release comes
When light which faith sheds
Consoles and comforts me.

Infinite Love

Torn by physical and mental agony;
Drifting and drowning
Amidst the sea of despair;
Struggling and surfacing for breath,
A straw I caught,
That gently wafted me,
To belief and safety.

The pain disappeared;
So did the nerve-racking fear;
Despair vanished,
Leaving behind
The naked, mire bespattered
Blood sodden, contrite soul;
Drenched in gratitude and praise.

Your infinite love once more proved,
Strengthened, the slushy, sin burdened soul-
Striving and struggling persistently
To erase imprints,
Human errors engraved upon it-
By the inexorable flow of worldly life.

&&&&&&&&&&& End &&&&&&&&&&&

Printed in the United States
By Bookmasters